GW00715868

To:

LYNN

From:

YOUR BEST FRIEND
MAM. X.

Date:

21 - 7 - 1906.

Message:

MY LOVE IS
INFINITE
FOR YOU
LYNN.

Friend to Friend

2002 © the Helen Steiner Rice Foundation – All rights reserved.

© 2002, Christian Art Gifts, P.O. Box 1599, Vereeniging, 1930, South Africa

Designed by Christian Art Gifts

ISBN 1-86852-950-9

Printed in Hong Kong

02 03 04 05 06 07 08 09 10 11 – 10 9 8 7 6 5 4 3 2 1

Friend
to friend

Tiny Treasures

HELEN STEINER RICE

Not only on New Year's,
but all year through,
God gives us a chance
to begin life anew.

LORD, I have heard of your fame;
I stand in awe of your deeds,
O LORD. Renew them in our day,
in our time make them known.

Habakkuk 3:2

This is the day to start anew.
With the beginning of a new year,
plan a personal renewal as well.

As the new year starts and the old year ends, there's no better time to make amends for all the things we sincerely regret and wish in our hearts we could somehow forget.

If you really change your ways and your actions ... then I will let you live in this place.
Jeremiah 7:5-7

This is the day to bid farewell to the year just ending and welcome the new one with its challenges and opportunities.

All of God's treasures
are yours to share
if you love Him completely
and show Him you care.

*We love because
he first loved us.*
1 John 4:19

This is the day to put another
log of friendship on the fire
and kindle the embers when you
sense a chill between two neighbors.
Acting as a peacemaker is
one of God's greatest treasures.

Accept what the new year brings, see-
ing the hand of God in all things, and
as you grow in strength and grace
the clearer you can see God's face.

Wealth and honor come from you;
you are the ruler of all things. In your
hands are strength and power ...
1 Chronicles 29:12-13

This is the day to marvel as
you discover a bit of God in people,
in nature and in happenings.

Suddenly, Lord,
I'm no longer afraid
my burden is lighter,
and the dark shadows fade.

Cast your cares on the LORD
and he will sustain you; he
will never let the righteous fall.
Psalm 55:22

This is the day to dismiss
all negative thinking and
concentrate on the positive.

You make me feel welcome,
You reach out Your hand,
I need never explain,
for You understand.

Accept one another, then,
just as Christ accepted you, in
order to bring praise to God.

Romans 15:7

This is the day to welcome Christ
into your home and your heart.
Your home and heart should always
have the welcome mat displayed.

We all make mistakes,
for it's human to err,
but no one need ever
give up in despair,
for God gives us all
a brand-new beginning,
a chance to start over
and repent of our sinning.

*Who is a God like you, who
pardons sin and forgives the transgression
of the remnant of his inheritance?*
Micah 7:18

"I'm sorry" can sound like music
to the ears of the one wronged.

As you start another year,
may you feel His presence near,
and may happiness that's heaven-sent
fill you heart with joy and content.

Surely you have granted him
eternal blessings and made him
glad with the joy of your presence.
Psalm 21:6

This is the day to apply yourself
wholeheartedly to the year
ahead and its tasks. The only
place that success comes
before work is in the dictionary.

Whatever the new year has in store,
remember,
there's always good reason for
everything that comes into our life,
even in times of struggle and strife.

My son, do not make light of
the Lord's discipline, and do not
lose heart when he rebukes you.
Hebrews 12:5

This is the day to remove
strife from your life by
adding giving to your living.

Only love can make man kind,
and kindness of heart brings
peace of mind, and by giving
love we can start this year
to lift the clouds of hate and fear.

Jesus replied, "If anyone loves me,
he will obey my teaching. My Father
will love him, and we will come to
him and make our home with him."
John 14:23

You can give yourself a lift
by raising the level of
kindness which you extend.

Everybody everywhere,
no matter what his station,
has moments of deep loneliness
and quiet desperation.

We are hard pressed on every side,
but not crushed; perplexed, but not in
despair; persecuted, but not abandoned;
struck down, but not destroyed.
2 Corinthians 4:8-9

This is the day to visit a friend
either in person or by telephone.

For things that cause the heart to ache
until we feel that it must break,
become the strength by which we climb
to higher heights that are sublime.

Therefore do not worry about
tomorrow, for tomorrow will
worry about itself. Each day
has enough trouble of its own.
Matthew 6:34

This is the day to help
someone up the hill of life. Be
a facilitator, an encourager.

Lord, I'm unworthy, I know,
but I do love You so –
I beg You to answer my plea ...
I've not much to give,
but as long as I live,
may I give it completely to Thee!

Listen to me, O LORD;
hear what my accusers are saying!
Jeremiah 18:19

This is the day to dedicate
your future to your Lord,
to give Him your present
and to offer up your past.

Make me a channel of blessing today,
I ask again and again when I pray –
do I turn a deaf ear
to the Master's voice
or refuse to heed
His directions and choice?

*Here I am! I stand at the door
and knock. If anyone hears my
voice and opens the door, I will come
in and eat with him, and he with me.*
Revelation 3:20

This is the day to
follow the Master's
directions. Listen to His voice.

Take a cup of kindness,
mix it well with love,
add a lot of patience
and faith in God above.

And if anyone gives even a cup of
cold water to one of these little ones
because he is my disciple, I tell you the
truth, he will certainly not lose his reward.
Matthew 10:42

This is the day to develop kindness.
It is closely related to greatness
and adds to the enjoyment of living
for you and those around you.

Start every day
with a "good morning" prayer
and God will bless each thing
you do and keep you in His care.

Every day I will praise you and extol
your name for ever and ever. Great
is the LORD and most worthy of praise;
his greatness no one can fathom.

Psalm 145:2-3

This is the day to make your
mornings good, your noons
better and your nights best
by placing them in God's care.

In Thy goodness and mercy
look down on this weak, erring one
and tell me that I am forgiven
for all I've so willfully done.

*If we confess our sins, he is faithful
and just and will forgive us our sins and
purify us from all unrighteousness.*
1 John 1:9

This is the day to hold
yourself accountable to the same
standards you demand of others.

Hour by hour and day by day
I talk to God and say when I pray,
"God, show me the way
so I know what to do,
I am willing and ready
if I just knew."

Then I heard the voice of the Lord saying,
"Whom shall I send? And who will go for
us?" And I said, "Here am I. Send me!"

Isaiah 6:8

This is the day to realize that every
problem has a solution and every
solution has a beginning. Ask God
to make you part of the solution.

How will you use the days of this year
and the time God
has placed in your hands –
will you waste the minutes
and squander the hours,
leaving no prints
behind in time's sands?

I tell you, now is the time
of God's favor, now is
the day of salvation.
2 Corinthians 6:2

This is the day to think
of time as a gift from God.
Appreciate each second.

Although we're unworthy,
dear Father above,
accept us today
and let us dwell in Thy love.

*I can do everything through
him who gives me strength.*
Philippians 4:13

This is the day to seek
residence in God's love and to invite
Jesus to reside in your heart.

Keep on believing, whatever betide you,
knowing that God
will be with you to guide you,
and all that He promised
will be yours to receive
if you trust Him completely
and always believe.

I will praise you forever for
what you have done; in your name
I will hope, for your name is good.
Psalm 52:9

This is the day to display a
faith that remains unshaken
despite the onset of tribulations.

Try a little better
and always be forgiving –
add a little sunshine
to the world in which we're living.

Then Peter came to Jesus and asked,
"Lord, how many times shall I forgive my
brother when he sins against me? Up to
seven times?" Jesus answered, "I tell you,
not seven times, but seventy-seven times.
Matthew 18:21, 22

This is the day to warm
the lives of those around you
by your Christlike attitude.

There are many things
in life we cannot understand,
but we must trust God's judgment
and be guided by His hand.

*Instead, he entrusted himself
to him who judges justly.*
1 Peter 2:23

This is the day to face
your problems with the
understanding that God has hidden
a blessing within each problem.

I come not to ask,
to plead or implore You –
I come just to tell You
how much I adore You,
for to kneel in Your presence
makes me feel blessed,
for I know that you know
all my needs best.

Praise be to the LORD, for
he has heard my cry for mercy.
Psalm 28:6

This is the day to listen to
your heart. Each beat is
a thank-you note to God.

Thank you again
for Your mercy and love
and for making me heir
to Your kingdom above!

*The LORD is my strength and my
shield; my heart trusts in him, and
I am helped. My heart leaps for joy and
I will give thanks to him in song.*

Psalm 28:7

This is the day to contemplate
your relationship with the Lord.

All who have God's blessing
can rest safely in His care,
for He promises safe passage
on the wings of faith and prayer.

I long to dwell in your tent
forever and take refuge in
the shelter of your wings.
Psalm 61:4

This is the day to proceed
on life's journey by travelling
with God as your co-pilot.

Whatever our problems,
our troubles and sorrows,
if we trust in the Lord,
there'll be brighter tomorrows.

I trust in God's unfailing
love for ever and ever.
Psalm 52:8

This is the day to be content in the
knowledge that God knows best.

I said a little prayer for you,
and I asked the Lord above
to keep you safely in His care
and enfold you in His love.

*If you remain in me and my
words remain in you, ask whatever you
wish, and it will be given you.*

John 15:7

This is the day to
experience God's
presence as you pray
for those you love.

Faith in things we cannot see
requires a child's simplicity –
oh, Father, grant once more to men
a simple, childlike faith again.

We live by faith, not by sight.
2 Corinthians 5:7

This is the day to confide in
Christ. Tell Him your faith is childlike, and your trust has matured.

Open up your hardened heart
and let God enter in –
He only wants to help you
a new life to begin.

Don't grumble against each other,
brothers, or you will be judged.
The Judge is standing at the door!
James 5:9

This is the day to answer
your heart's door chime.
God is waiting. Ask Him in.

When God forgives us, we too
must forgive and resolve to do
better each day that we live by
constantly trying to be like Him
more nearly and trust in His
wisdom and love Him more dearly.

*Bear with each other and forgive whatever
grievances you may have against one
another. Forgive as the Lord forgave you.*
Colossians 3:13

This is the day to imitate Jesus.
Forgive someone who has
hurt you. Turn the other cheek.

"Love one another as I have loved you"
may seem impossible to do,
but if you will try to trust and believe,
great are the joys that you will receive.

I have told you this so that
my joy may be in you and
that your joy may be complete.
John 15:11

This is the day to be a living
sermon for the people in your life.
It is far more meaningful for them
to see a sermon than to hear one.

After the night, the morning,
bidding all darkness cease,
after life's cares and sorrows,
the comfort and sweetness of peace.

The LORD watches over you — the
LORD is your shade at your right
hand; the sun will not harm
you by day, nor the moon by night.
Psalm 121:5-6

This is the day to thank your
Creator for your hopes, your dreams
and your faith in what is to come.

God, how little I am really aware
of the pain and the trouble
and deep despair
that flood the hearts
of those in pain
as they struggle to cope
but feel it's in vain.

Wait for the LORD; be strong and
take heart and wait for the LORD.
Psalm 27:14

This is the day to look beyond the be-
havior of that unpleasant individual.
Analyze why the unkind words were
spoken. Be understanding.

God, in Thy great wisdom
lead us in the way that's right,
and may the darkness of this world
be conquered by Thy light.

I have come into the world
as a light, so that no one who believes
in me should stay in darkness.
John 12:46

This is the day to recharge your
spiritual generator. Request the Light
of the world to illuminate your way.

Let me stop complaining
about my load of care,
for God will always lighten it
when it gets too much to bear.

*When anxiety was great
within me, your consolation
brought joy to my soul.*
Psalm 94:19

This is the day to
handle yourself by
using your head.
Handle others by
using your heart.

May you find comfort
in the thought that sorrow,
grief and woe are sent into our lives
sometimes to help our souls to grow.

*The law of the LORD is perfect, reviving
the soul. The statutes of the LORD are
trustworthy, making wise the simple.*
Psalm 19:7

This is the day to cultivate an
attitude of assistance. If a neighbor
experiences a sorrow, be the first one
to ask, "What can I do to help?"

The Lord is our salvation
and our strength in every fight,
our redeemer and protector,
our eternal guiding light.

*Come, O house of Jacob, let us
walk in the light of the Lord.*
Isaiah 2:5

This is the day to protect someone's
reputation if you hear malicious
gossip. Guide the conversation to a
higher level. Discourage rumors.

God enters the heart
that is broken with sorrow
as He opens the door
to a brighter tomorrow,
for only through tears
can we recognize the suffering
that lies in another's eyes.

*Why are you downcast, O my soul ...
Put your hope in God, for I will yet
praise him, my Savior and my God.*

Psalm 43:5

This is the day to
improve self-esteem in an
individual who is lacking it.

Earthly pain is never too much
when He bestows His merciful touch,
and if you look to Him and pray,
He will help you through every day.

For everyone born of God overcomes
the world. This is the victory that
has overcome the world, even our faith.
1 John 5:4

This is the day to avoid
complaining. Appreciate
even the smallest of
courtesies extended to you.

It does not take a special time
to make a brand-new start,
it only takes the deep desire
to try with all our heart.

But the man who looks intently into
the perfect law that gives freedom,
and continues to do this, not forgetting
what he has heard, but doing it —
he will be blessed in what he does.
James 1:25

This is the day to exchange some
negative habits for more productive
ones. Put them into action. Practice
and persevere at being a doer!

There's no need at all
for impressive prayer,
for the minute we seek God,
He is already there!

Pray to your Father, who is unseen.
Then your Father, who sees
what is done in secret, will reward you.
Matthew 6:6

This is the day to engage in
pleasant conversation with God.

After the clouds, the sunshine,
after the winter, the spring,
after the shower, the rainbow,
for life is a changeable thing.

*Whenever I bring clouds over the earth and
the rainbow appears in the clouds, I will
remember my covenant between me and you
and all living creatures of every kind.*
Genesis 9:14-15

This is the day to
change someone's life
by acting as a rainbow.

Love makes us patient,
understanding and kind,
and we judge with our hearts
and not with our minds,
for as soon as love enters
the heart's open door
the faults we once saw
are not there anymore.

Love must be sincere.
Romans 12:9

This is the day to bring out
the best in another person.

Love is like magic,
and it always will be,
for love still remains
life's sweet mystery!

God is love. Whoever lives in
love lives in God, and God in him.
1 John 4:16

This is the day to influence
someone's life by demonstrating
the magic of love; after all, it is love
that makes the world go round.

Shed Thy light upon us
as Easter dawns this year,
and may we feel the presence
of the risen Savior near.

It is true! The Lord has risen ...
Luke 24:34

This is the day to rise above the
pettiness that is prevalent in society
today. Let your own light shine.

He who walked by the Galilee
touched the blind and made them see
and cured the man who long was lame,
when they but called God's holy name.

*Then will the eyes of the blind be
opened and the ears of the deaf unstopped.
Then will the lame leap like a deer,
and the mute tongue shout for joy.*
Isaiah 35:5-6

This is the day to strive to do
something constructive. Put
forth an effort to right a wrong.

Take me and break me and make me,
dear God, just what
you want me to be –
give me the strength
to accept what you send
and eyes with the vision to see.

*But the Lord stood at my side and gave
me strength, so that through me the
message might be fully proclaimed ...*
2 Timothy 4:17

This is the day to possess
a vision of hope. Apply
action to your dream. With God's
help it will come to fruition.

~ 52 ~

Teach us to take time for praying
and to find time for listening to You,
so each day is spent well and wisely
doing what You most want us to do.

Watch and pray so that you will
not fall into temptation. The spirit
is willing, but the body is weak.
Matthew 26:41

This is the day to prioritize
your responsibilities. Be
well-adjusted spiritually, physically,
mentally and emotionally.

Trouble is something
no one can escape,
everyone has it in
some form or shape.

Then they cried to the LORD
in their trouble, and he
saved them from their distress.
Psalm 107:13

This is the day to value the
existence of trouble. It
strengthens your coping skills.

Uncover before me
my weakness and greed
and help me to search
deep inside so I may discover
how easy it is
to be selfishly lost in my pride.

Pride goes before destruction,
a haughty spirit before a fall.
Proverbs 16:18

This is the day to be concerned
about others. Plan to serve God
first, then others and then yourself.

I wish I could wipe away
every trace of pain
and suffering from your face,
but He is great and we are small,
we just can't alter His will at all.

*He will wipe every tear from their
eyes. There will be no more death or
mourning or crying or pain, for the old
order of things has passed away.*
Revelation 21:4

This is the day to enjoy a beauty
treatment. Remove the frown
from your face and add a smile.

Never give up in despair and think that you are through, for there's always a tomorrow and a chance to start anew.

You were taught, with regard to your former way of life, to put off your old self, which is being corrupted by its deceitful desires; to be made new in the attitude of your minds; and to put on the new self, created to be like God in true righteousness and holiness.

Ephesians 4:22-24

This is the day to learn
from each person you meet
and from each happening.

Just keep on smiling,
whatever betide you,
secure in the knowledge
God is always beside you.

*When I smiled at them,
they scarcely believed it; the light
of my face was precious to them.*
Job 29:24

This is the day to share
the secret of a truly happy
life. Encourage the talent
within a youngster.

God has promised to sustain us,
He's our refuge from all harms,
and underneath this refuge
are His everlasting arms!

The eternal God is your refuge, and
underneath are the everlasting arms.

Deuteronomy 33:27

This is the day to study a
crucifix. Observe that even
on the cross Christ's arms
are open wide in welcome.

My cross is not too heavy,
my road is not too rough,
because God walks beside me,
and to know this is enough.

When you pass through the waters,
I will be with you; and when you
pass through the rivers, they will
not sweep over you. When you walk
through the fire, you will not be burned;
the flames will not set you ablaze.

Isaiah 43:2

This is the day to travel the rough roads
and traumatic times with God beside you.

Though I'm tired and weary
and I wish my race were run,
God will only terminate it
when my work on earth is done.

*I have fought the good
fight, I have finished the race,
I have kept the faith.*
2 Timothy 4:7

This is the day to polish your trophy
called compassion, a humanitarian
award conceived by God for those
who alleviate the suffering of others.

Miracles are all around
within our sight and touch and sound,
as true and wonderful today
as when the stone was rolled away.

... they asked each other, "Who will
roll the stone away from the entrance
of the tomb?" But when they looked
up, they saw that the stone, which was
very large, had been rolled away.
Mark 16:2-4

This is the day to put
your shoulder to the
stone of indifference.

Seed must be sown
to bring forth grain,
and nothing is born
without suffering and pain.

*Now he who supplies seed to the sower
and bread for food will also supply and
increase your store of seed and will
enlarge the harvest of your righteousness.*
2 Corinthians 9:10

This is the day to reap that
which you have sown. Did you
plant seeds of kindness? Then
harvest a bushel of kindnesses.

When our lives are overcast
with trouble and with care,
give us faith to see beyond
the dark clouds of despair.

Therefore I tell you, do
not worry about your life.
Matthew 6:25

This is the day to mature and
grow in grace. The sun is hiding
behind the clouds, and your frown
is a smile turned upside-down.

Flowers sleeping peacefully
beneath the winter's snow
awaken from their icy grave
when spring winds start to blow.

*Therefore we do not lose heart. Though
outwardly we are wasting away, yet
inwardly we are being renewed day by day.*
2 Corinthians 4:16

This is the day to look for
and discover hidden possibilities.
Bring out the dormant potential
within another person.

Be glad that you've walked
with courage each day,
be glad you've had strength
for each step of the way,
be glad for the comfort
you've found in prayer,
but be gladdest of all
for God's tender care.

Rejoice in the LORD and be glad, you righteous; sing, all you who are upright in heart!
Psalm 32:11

This is the day to stroll with a
confident air. Jesus is at your side
teaching you to walk as He walked.

The bleakness of the winter
is melted by the sun.
The tree that looked so stark
and dead becomes a living one.

Water will gush forth in the
wilderness and streams in the desert.
Isaiah 35:6

This is the day to melt any
hardness in your heart. Reach
out in forgiveness. Life goes on.

May I stand undaunted
come what may,
secure in the knowledge
I have only to pray
and ask my Creator
and Father above
to keep me serene
in His grace and His love!

*If you believe, you will receive
whatever you ask for in prayer.*
Matthew 21:22

This is the day to remain calm
in the face of all adversities.

How can man feel any fear of doubt
when on every side,
all around and about,
the March winds blow
across man's face
and whisper of God's power and grace.

By his breath the skies became fair;
his hand pierced the gliding serpent.
Job 26:13

This is the day to renew
your amazement at the power
and majesty of God. It is
no secret what He can do.

God, be my resting place and my
protection in hours of trouble, defeat
and dejection, may I never give way
to self-pity and sorrow, may I always
be sure of a better tomorrow.

*Every word of God is flawless; he is a
shield to those who take refuge in him.*
Proverbs 30:5

This is the day to use all
twenty-four hours to make
the most of yourself, because
there will never be another you.

God, open my eyes
so I may see and feel
Your presence close to me,
give me strength for my stumbling feet
as I battle the crowd
on life's busy street.

*Now we see but a poor reflection as
in a mirror; then we shall see face to
face. Now I know in part; then I shall
know fully, even as I am fully known.*
1 Corinthians 13:12

Do not concentrate on the physical
features, but rather the inner beauty.
Are you pleased with what you see?

Widen my vision of unseeing eyes,
so in passing faces I'll recognize
not just a stranger, unloved and unknown,
but a friend with a heart
that is much like my own.

*Then he turned to his disciples
and said privately, "Blessed are
the eyes that see what you see."*
Luke 10:23

You cannot judge a book by its
cover, and do not judge a person
by the garments being worn.

Love works in ways that are wondrous and strange, and there is nothing in life that love cannot change, and all that God promised will someday come true when you love one another the way He loved you.

Now remain in my love. If you obey my commands, you will remain in my love, just as I have obeyed my Father's commands and remain in his love.
John 15:9-10

This is the day to treat all those with whom you have contact as you wish they would treat you.

Happiness is giving up
wishing for things we have not
and making the best
of whatever we've got –
it's knowing that life
is determined for us
and pursuing our tasks
without fret, fume or fuss.

*But godliness with contentment is great
gain. For we brought nothing into the
world, and we can take nothing out of it.*
1 Timothy 6:6-7

This is the day to do the job
assigned to you really well.

Let us face the trouble
that is ours this present minute
and count on God to help us
and to put His mercy in it.

The Lord disciplines those he loves.
Hebrews 12:6

This is the day to introduce the
word "help" into your vocabulary.
Help yourself, help others,
and thank God for His help.

By completing
what God gives us to do,
we find real contentment
and happiness too.

That is why, for Christ's sake, I
delight in weaknesses, in insults, in
hardships, in persecutions, in difficulties.
For when I am weak, then I am strong.
2 Corinthians 12:10

This is the day to look for
the many available oppportunities
to serve God. Don't wait
for big, exceptional chances,
but use small, daily occasions.

Enjoy your sojourn
on earth and be glad
that God gives you a choice
between good things and bad,
and only be sure
that you heed God's voice
whenever life asks you
to make a choice.

Today, if you hear his voice,
do not harden your hearts.
Hebrews 3:7-8

This is the day to banish gloom
and add cheer to somebody's life.
Replace sadness with gladness.

God's love knows no exceptions,
so never feel excluded –
no matter who or what you are,
your name has been included.

Let your face shine on your servant;
save me in your unfailing love.
Psalm 31:16

This is the day to
discover the really important
things in your life.

Forget the past and future
and dwell wholly on today.
For God controls the future,
and He will direct our way.

There is a future for the man of peace.
Psalm 37:37

This is the day to call to
mind the saying, "Today is the first
day of the rest of your life."

Give me perception to make
me aware that scattered
profusely on life's thoroughfare
are the best gifts of God that
we daily pass by as we look at
the world with an unseeing eye.

However, as it is written: "No
eye has seen, no ear has heard,
no mind has conceived what God has
prepared for those who love him."
1 Corinthians 2:9

This is the day to describe
the sunrise or sunset to
someone who cannot see it.

Our Father Who art in heaven,
hear this little prayer,
and reach across the miles today
that stretch from here to there.

Our Father in heaven,
hallowed be your name.
Matthew 6:9

This is the day to write a letter
of affirmation to someone.

Happiness is waking up
and beginning the day
by counting our blessings
and kneeling to pray.

*Blessed are the people of whom
this is true; blessed are the
people whose God is the* LORD.
Psalm 144:15

This is the day to wake up
singing and improve your outlook.

After the winter comes the spring
to show us that in everything
there's always renewal divinely planned,
flawlessly perfect,
the work of God's hand.

Jesus said to her, "I am the resurrection
and the life. He who believes in
me will live, even though he dies;
and whoever lives and believes in me
will never die. Do you believe this?"
John 11:26

This is the day to admire the divine
plan that promises life ever after.

No matter what your past has been,
trust God to understand,
and no matter what your problem is,
just place it in His hand.

Forget the former things;
do not dwell on the past.
Isaiah 43:18

This is the day to dismiss unfair
criticism that is directed at
you. Learn to accept it as Jesus
did. Shoulder it and carry on.

If you walk in Christ's footsteps
and have faith to believe
there's nothing you ask
for that you will not receive!

To this you were called, because Christ
suffered for you, leaving you an example,
that you should follow in his steps.
1 Peter 2:21

This is the day to think about the
Indian and his moccasins, for
"until you walk in the shoes of the
other person, don't judge him".

When we view our problems
through the eyes of God above,
misfortunes turn to blessings,
and hatred turns to love.

*You will seek me and find me
when you seek me with all your heart.*
Jeremiah 29:13

This is the day to display
your sense of humor.
A strong faith in God permits
you to laugh at yourself,
but never at others.

Man, like flowers, too must sleep
until he is called
from the darkened deep
to live in that place where angels sing
and where there is eternal spring!

For a time is coming when all
who are in their graves will
hear his voice and come out.
John 5:28-29

This is the day to go forth
and spread the good news.

Little brooks and singing streams, icebound beneath the snow, begin to babble merrily beneath the sun's warm glow, and all around on every side new life and joy appear to tell us nothing ever dies and we should have no fear.

So we fix our eyes not on what is seen, but on what is unseen. For what is seen is temporary, but what is unseen is eternal.
2 Corinthians 4:18

This is the day to defrost your icy attitude. Warm someone's life with a little laughter.

Remember, when you're troubled
with uncertainty and doubt,
it is best to tell your Father
what your fear is all about.

*"For I know the plans I have for
you," declares the LORD, "plans to
prosper you and not to harm you,
plans to give you hope and a future."*
Jeremiah 29:11

This is the day to change
the world by starting with your
own attitude and actions.

I know God made a special
cross for me, for in His great
wisdom He knew what I could
not see – often the loveliest
crosses are the heaviest crosses to
bear, for only God is wise enough
to choose the cross we can wear.

*Then Jesus said to his disciples, "If anyone
would come after me, he must deny himself
and take up his cross and follow me."*
Matthew 16:24

This is the day to shoulder
your cross. Christ did.

God, grant us grace to use
all the hours of our days
not for our own selfish interests
and our own willful ways.

Then he returned to his disciples
and found them sleeping. "Could
you men not keep watch with
me for one hour?" he asked Peter.
Matthew 26:40

This is the day to be helpful. You
will find that the degree of happiness
you achieve is directly related to
the degree of helpfulness you offer.

Life's lovely garden
would be sweeter by far
if all who passed through
it were as nice as you are.

See! The winter is past; the rains are
over and gone. Flowers appear on the
earth; the season of singing has come,
the cooing of doves is heard in our land.
Song of Solomon 2:11-12

This is the day to meet Jesus in the
garden. Walk and talk with Him.

In the glorious Easter story a troubled
world can find blessed reassurance
and enduring peace of mind.

*"Don't be alarmed," he said. "You
are looking for Jesus the Nazarene, who
was crucified. He has risen! He is not
here. See the place where they laid him."*
Mark 16:6

This is the day to harmonize with
nature's orchestra. Crickets chirp,
brooks babble, flowers and trees
sway to the rhythm of the symphony
of praise to our Savior. Even
thunder adds a clap of applause.

Our Savior's resurrection
was God's way of telling men
that in Christ we are eternal
and in Him we live again.

*For my Father's will is that everyone
who looks to the Son and believes
in him shall have eternal life, and
I will raise him up at the last day.*
John 6:40

This is the day to rejoice in the
realization that our earthly cares and
sorrows are minimal when compared
to the reward of eternal life.

Everything worth having
demands work and sacrifice,
and freedom is a gift from God
that commands the highest price.

It is for freedom that Christ has set us free.
Stand firm, then, and do not let yourselves
be burdened again by a yoke of slavery.
Galatians 5:1

This is the day to value the
freedoms you enjoy daily.

My blessings are so many,
my troubles are so few,
how can I feel discouraged
when I know that I have You.

Be strong and courageous.
Do not be terrified; do not be
discouraged, for the LORD your God
will be with you wherever you go.
Joshua 1:9

This is the day to display a spiritual
magnetism. Attract others to Jesus
by your example of positive faith.